EASY CHICKEN

BREAST COOKBOOK

50 UNIQUE AND EASY CHICKEN BREAST RECIPES

2nd Edition

By
BookSumo Press

Published by
BookSumo Press, a DBA of Saxonberg Associates
http://www.booksumo.com/

ABOUT THE AUTHOR.

BookSumo Press is a publisher of unique, easy, and healthy cookbooks.

Our cookbooks span all topics and all subjects. If you want a deep dive into the possibilities of cooking with any type of ingredient. Then BookSumo Press is your go to place for robust yet simple and delicious cookbooks and recipes. Whether you are looking for great tasting pressure cooker recipes or authentic ethic and cultural food. BookSumo Press has a delicious and easy cookbook for you.

With simple ingredients, and even simpler step-by-step instructions BookSumo cookbooks get everyone in the kitchen chefing delicious meals.

BookSumo is an independent publisher of books operating in the beautiful Garden State (NJ) and our team of chefs and kitchen experts are here to teach, eat, and be merry!

INTRODUCTION

Welcome to *The Effortless Chef Series*! Thank you for taking the time to purchase this cookbook.

Come take a journey into the delights of easy cooking. The point of this cookbook and all BookSumo Press cookbooks is to exemplify the effortless nature of cooking simply.

In this book we focus on cooking with chicken breasts. You will find that even though the recipes are simple, the taste of the dishes are quite amazing.

So will you take an adventure in simple cooking? If the answer is yes please consult the table of contents to find the dishes you are most interested in.

Once you are ready, jump right in and start cooking.

— BookSumo Press

TABLE OF CONTENTS

Any Issues? Contact Us

If you find that something important to you is missing from this book please contact us at info@booksumo.com.

We will take your concerns into consideration when the 2nd edition of this book is published. And we will keep you updated!

— BookSumo Press

LEGAL NOTES

COMMON ABBREVIATIONS

cup(s)	C.
tablespoon	tbsp
teaspoon	tsp
ounce	oz.
pound	lb

*All units used are standard American measurements

Chapter 1: Easy Chicken Breast Recipes

Restaurant Style Chicken Breast

Ingredients

- 6 skinless, boneless chicken breast halves
- 1/4 C. all-purpose flour
- 1/2 tsp salt
- 1 pinch ground black pepper
- 3 tbsps butter
- 1 (14.5 oz.) can stewed tomatoes, with liquid
- 1/2 C. water
- 2 tbsps brown sugar
- 2 tbsps distilled white vinegar
- 2 tbsps Worcestershire sauce
- 1 tsp salt
- 2 tsps chili powder
- 1 tsp mustard powder
- 1/2 tsp celery seed
- 1 clove garlic, minced
- 1/8 tsp hot pepper sauce

Directions

- Get a bowl, mix: black pepper, flour, and half a tsp of salt.
- Coat your chicken with this mix then brown the outsides of the chicken in butter.
- Place your chicken to the side.

- After you have browned all the chicken, in the same pan, add in: hot sauce, tomatoes, garlic, water, celery seed, brown sugar, mustard, vinegar, chili powder, and Worcestershire sauce.
- Get the mix boiling and once it is, add the chicken back in to the sauce.
- Get everything boiling again and then place a lid on the pan, set the heat to low, and let the chicken gently cook for 37 mins, until it is fully done.
- Let the contents cool before serving.
- Enjoy.

Amount per serving (6 total)

Timing Information:

Preparation	30 m
Cooking	40 m
Total Time	1 h 10 m

Nutritional Information:

Calories	247 kcal
Fat	7.8 g
Carbohydrates	14.8g
Protein	28.8 g
Cholesterol	84 mg
Sodium	915 mg

* Percent Daily Values are based on a 2,000 calorie diet.

LEMON PEPPER AND MONTEREY CHICKEN

Ingredients

- 4 (6 oz.) skinless, boneless chicken breast halves
- 1/4 tsp salt
- 1/4 tsp lemon pepper seasoning
- 1 tbsp vegetable oil
- 8 strips bacon
- 1 onion, sliced
- 1/4 C. packed brown sugar
- 1/2 C. shredded Colby-Monterey Jack cheese

Directions

- Coat your chicken pieces with lemon pepper and salt before stir frying them in oil for 14 mins, until fully done. Once finished place your chicken to the side.
- Fry your bacon in the same pot for 11 mins and then place them to the side on some paper towels.
- Add in your onions to the bacon fat and stir fry them for 7 mins.
- To serve your chicken wrap each piece with two pieces of bacon and then add a topping of onions and cheese.
- Enjoy.

Amount per serving (4 total)

Timing Information:

Preparation	5 m
Cooking	30 m
Total Time	35 m

Nutritional Information:

Calories	431 kcal
Fat	20.1 g
Carbohydrates	16.9g
Protein	44 g
Cholesterol	124 mg
Sodium	809 mg

* Percent Daily Values are based on a 2,000 calorie diet.

Stuffed Chicken Breast I
(Sun Dried Tomatoes, Feta, and Spinach)

Ingredients

- 6 skinless, boneless chicken breast halves, flattened
- 1 (8 oz.) bottle Italian-style salad dressing
- 8 slices of stale wheat bread, torn
- 3/4 C. grated Parmesan cheese
- 1 tsp chopped fresh thyme
- 1/8 tsp pepper
- 1 1/2 C. feta cheese, crumbled
- 1/2 C. sour cream
- 1 tbsp vegetable oil
- 3 cloves garlic, minced
- 4 C. chopped fresh spinach
- 1 bunch green onions, chopped
- 1 C. mushrooms, sliced
- 1 (8 oz.) jar oil-packed sun-dried tomatoes, chopped

Directions

- Marinate your chicken in dressing for 1 hr in the fridge.
- Now blend the following: pepper, bread, thyme, and parmesan.

- Make bread crumbs through pulsing the contents multiple times.
- Get a bowl, combine: sour cream and feta.
- Stir fry your garlic and spinach until the spinach is soft then add in the green onions and cook for 4 mins.
- Place the spinach on a plate and then add in your mushrooms and cook everything until it is all tender.
- Add the mushrooms to a plate with the spinach and let it cool.
- Once cool add everything to the feta mix. Then add the sundried tomatoes.
- Pour everything on a baking sheet and then place the sheet in the freezer for 35 mins.
- Now set your oven to 400 degrees before doing anything else.
- Get your chicken pieces and put them in a casserole dish with an equal amount of filling placed on the middle of each.
- Roll up the chicken and stake a toothpick through each one.
- Top with the blended bread and cook everything in oven for 30 mins.
- Enjoy.

Amount per serving (6 total)

Timing Information:

Preparation	1 h
Cooking	45 m
Total Time	2 h 45 m

Nutritional Information:

Calories	633 kcal
Fat	35.9 g
Carbohydrates	34.8g
Protein	44.4 g
Cholesterol	121 mg
Sodium	1555 mg

* Percent Daily Values are based on a 2,000 calorie diet.

PINEAPPLE, BROWN SUGAR, AND ONION CHICKEN

Ingredients

- 10 skinless, boneless chicken breast halves
- 2 C. dry bread crumbs
- 2 tbsps all-purpose flour
- 1 tbsp dried oregano
- 2 tsps salt
- 2 tsps ground black pepper
- 1 tbsp vegetable oil
- 1 1/2 C. packed brown sugar
- 1/4 C. prepared mustard
- 1/2 C. ketchup
- 1 tbsp Worcestershire sauce
- 1 tbsp soy sauce
- 1/4 C. grated onion
- 1/2 tsp salt
- 3/4 C. water
- 10 pineapple rings

Directions

- Clean your chicken under cold water and then add them to a bowl with: pepper, salt (2 tbsps), flour, and bread crumbs.
- Make sure all the chicken pieces are evenly coated.
- Set your oven to 350 degrees before doing anything else.
- For 5 mins on each side fry your chicken, in oil, in a frying pan.

- Then add them to a casserole dish that has been coated with nonstick spray or oil.
- Get a big pot and get the following boiling for 3 mins: water, brown sugar, half a tsp of salt, mustard, onions, ketchup, soy sauce, and Worcestershire.
- Now top your chicken with the boiling mixture and then cook everything in the oven for 60 mins.
- When 5 mins is left in the cooking time put a piece of pineapple on each piece of chicken.
- Enjoy.

Amount per serving (10 total)

Timing Information:

Preparation	15 m
Cooking	1 h
Total Time	1 h 15 m

Nutritional Information:

Calories	425 kcal
Fat	4.4 g
Carbohydrates	65.3g
Protein	31.1 g
Cholesterol	68 mg
Sodium	1142 mg

* Percent Daily Values are based on a 2,000 calorie diet.

EASY ITALIAN SEASONED CHICKEN BREAST

Ingredients

- 2 large bone-in chicken breast halves with skin
- 1/4 C. extra-virgin olive oil
- 1/2 tsp garlic, minced
- 1/2 tsp coarse sea salt
- 1/2 tsp cracked black pepper
- 1/4 tsp dried rosemary
- 1/4 tsp dried basil

Directions

- Coat your chicken with: basil, olive oil, rosemary, garlic, black pepper, and salt.
- Then place them in a casserole dish and put everything in the fridge for 50 mins.
- Now set your oven to 375 degrees before doing anything else.
- Cook the chicken in the oven for 1 hr.
- Enjoy.

Amount per serving (2 total)

Timing Information:

Preparation	10 m
Cooking	45 m
Total Time	1 h 40 m

Nutritional Information:

Calories	615 kcal
Fat	42.2 g
Carbohydrates	0.7g
Protein	54.5 g
Cholesterol	1153 mg
Sodium	570 mg

* Percent Daily Values are based on a 2,000 calorie diet.

Stuffed Chicken Breast II
(Bacon, Garlic, and Feta)

Ingredients

- 1/2 C. mayonnaise
- 1 (10 oz.) package frozen chopped spinach, thawed and drained
- 1/2 C. crumbled feta cheese
- 2 cloves garlic, chopped
- 4 skinless, boneless chicken breasts
- 4 slices turkey bacon

Directions

- Set your oven to 375 degrees before doing anything else.
- Get a bowl, combine: garlic, mayo, feta, and spinach.
- Butterfly your chicken pieces to fill them with an equal amount of mixture. Roll back up your chicken pieces and wrap each one with a piece of bacon before staking each with a toothpick.
- Add your chicken rolls to a casserole dish and place a covering of foil around the dish.
- Cook everything in the oven for 60 mins and check that the internal temp of the chicken is 165 degrees. Enjoy.

Amount per serving (4 total)

Timing Information:

Preparation	25 m
Cooking	1 h
Total Time	1 h 25 m

Nutritional Information:

Calories	449 kcal
Fat	32.8 g
Carbohydrates	5.2g
Protein	33.4 g
Cholesterol	104 mg
Sodium	685 mg

* Percent Daily Values are based on a 2,000 calorie diet.

LEMON, DIJON, AND ROSEMARY CHICKEN

Ingredients

- 8 cloves garlic, minced
- 3 tbsps olive oil
- 2 tbsps minced fresh rosemary
- 1 1/2 tbsps Dijon mustard
- 1 1/2 tbsps lemon juice
- 1/4 tsp ground black pepper
- 1/8 tsp kosher salt
- 4 boneless, skinless chicken breast halves

Directions

- Heat up your grill and then coat the grate with some oil.
- Get a bowl, combine: salt, garlic, black pepper, olive oil, lemon juice, rosemary, and mustard.
- Marinate your chicken in this mix for 35 mins, after placing 1/8 of a C. of the marinade to the side for later.
- After the chicken has marinated cook it on the grill for 5 mins then flip it and coat the opposite side with the marinade that was reserved and cook for 6 more mins.
  Cover each piece of chicken with some foil and then let it sit for 5 mins to the side.
- Enjoy.

Amount per serving (4 total)

Timing Information:

Preparation	35 m
Cooking	10 m
Total Time	50 m

Nutritional Information:

Calories	232 kcal
Fat	11.6 g
Carbohydrates	3.9g
Protein	26.7 g
Cholesterol	66 mg
Sodium	276 mg

* Percent Daily Values are based on a 2,000 calorie diet.

Easy Flame Broiled Chicken Breast

Ingredients

- 3 tbsps extra virgin olive oil
- 4 bone-in chicken breast halves with skin
- 2 tsps kosher salt
- 1 tsp freshly ground black pepper

Directions

- Turn on your broiler and get it hot, make sure that the rack is at least 6 inches from the source of heat.
- Coat your chicken pieces with pepper, salt, and olive oil and put the skin side downwards on a broiling pan.
- Cook everything in the broiler for 11 mins then turn over the chicken and cook for 11 more mins.
- Check the internal temp of the chicken. It should be 165 degrees.
- Before serving the chicken let it sit for 10 mins.
- Enjoy.

Amount per serving (4 total)

Timing Information:

Preparation	5 m
Cooking	20 m
Total Time	30 m

Nutritional Information:

Calories	389 kcal
Fat	21.9 g
Carbohydrates	0.3g
Protein	45 g
Cholesterol	127 mg
Sodium	1067 mg

* Percent Daily Values are based on a 2,000 calorie diet.

Easy Italian Style Chicken Breast

Ingredients

- 1 1/2 C. shredded Italian cheese blend
- 1 clove garlic, finely chopped
- 1 tsp dried basil
- 1 tsp dried oregano
- 1/2 C. grated Parmesan cheese
- 1/2 C. Italian-seasoned bread crumbs
- 4 boneless, skinless chicken breasts
- 1 egg, well beaten
- 1 C. spaghetti sauce
- 1/4 C. shredded Italian cheese blend, or to taste (optional)

Directions

- Set your oven to 350 degrees before doing anything else.
- Get a bowl, mix: oregano, 1.5 C. of cheese, basil, and garlic.
- Get a 2nd bowl, mix: bread crumbs, and parmesan.
- Butterfly your chicken and then with a mallet flatten it out on a cutting board.

- Divide your mix equally amongst your pieces of chicken placing it in the center of the meat.
- Then the roll up the chicken around the cheese mix and coat the outside with some egg.
- Dip the roll into the parmesan mix and then place everything into a casserole dish that has been coated with nonstick spray.
- Cook the chicken in the oven for 50 mins.
- After the chicken is fully done top it with the pasta sauce and a quarter of a C. of Italian cheese.
- Cook everything for 7 more mins in the oven.
- Enjoy.

Amount per serving (4 total)

Timing Information:

Preparation	20 m
Cooking	50 m
Total Time	1 h 10 m

Nutritional Information:

Calories	470 kcal
Fat	22.7 g
Carbohydrates	21.5g
Protein	43.5 g
Cholesterol	154 mg
Sodium	1008 mg

* Percent Daily Values are based on a 2,000 calorie diet.

Stuffed Chicken Breast III

(Easy Creole Style)

Ingredients

- 1/2 lb smoked sausage, sliced thinly
- 1/2 lb fresh button mushrooms
- 3 tbsps chopped green onion
- 1 tsp minced garlic
- 4 tbsps blue cheese salad dressing, divided
- 3 skinless, boneless chicken breasts
- 1 tbsp Cajun-style seasoning

Directions

- Stir fry your sausage until browned all over then add in your mushrooms and continue stirring and frying for 7 mins.
- Now add in: garlic and green onions.
- Cook for 4 more mins.
- Now place this mix in a bowl and process it in a food processor or blender with 1 tbsp of dressing.

- Set your oven to 375 degrees before doing anything else.
- Slice an opening in your chicken and then place an equal amount of mushroom mix in each.
- Coat the chicken pieces with Cajun seasoning and then brown the outsides in a pan, in oil, for about 2 mins each side.
- Once the chicken has been fully browned add everything to a casserole dish and then cover them with the leftover mushroom mix (if any remains), and also any dressing.
- Cook everything in the oven for 35 mins, until the meat is fully done.
- Let the chicken sit for 10 mins before serving.
- Enjoy.

Amount per serving (3 total)

Timing Information:

Preparation	5 m
Cooking	55 m
Total Time	1 h

Nutritional Information:

Calories	553 kcal
Fat	36.5 g
Carbohydrates	7.5g
Protein	47.7 g
Cholesterol	123 mg
Sodium	1914 mg

* Percent Daily Values are based on a 2,000 calorie diet.

CREAM OF CHICKEN, STUFFING, AND SWISS

Ingredients

- 4 skinless, boneless chicken breast halves
- 8 slices Swiss cheese
- 1 (10.75 oz.) can cream of chicken soup
- 1/2 C. white wine
- 1 C. herb-seasoned stuffing mix, crushed
- 1/4 C. melted butter

Directions

- Set your oven to 350 degrees before doing anything else.
- Get a bowl, combine: wine, soup, and melted butter.
- Layer your chicken in a casserole dish and top with two pieces of cheese, and then the wine mix, and them some stuffing.
- Bake for 60 mins.
- Enjoy.

Amount per serving (4 total)

Timing Information:

Preparation	15 m
Cooking	55 m
Total Time	1 h 10 m

Nutritional Information:

Calories	730 kcal
Fat	36.1 g
Carbohydrates	47.4g
Protein	46.3 g
Cholesterol	154 mg
Sodium	1543 mg

* Percent Daily Values are based on a 2,000 calorie diet.

ONIONS, BACON, AND BROWN SUGAR CHICKEN BREAST

Ingredients

- 1/2 C. all-purpose flour
- 1/4 C. seasoned bread crumbs
- 2 tsps garlic salt
- 1 tsp freshly ground black pepper
- 4 (6 oz.) skinless, boneless chicken breast halves, flattened
- 8 turkey bacon strips
- 1 onion, sliced
- 1/4 tsp lemon-pepper seasoning
- 1/4 tsp Italian seasoning
- 1/4 tsp salt
- 1/8 tsp red pepper flakes, or more to taste
- 1/4 C. packed brown sugar
- 1/2 C. shredded Colby-Monterey Jack cheese

Directions

- Get a bowl, combine: black pepper, flour, garlic salt, and bread crumbs.
- Cover your chicken with this mix.
- Fry your bacon for 10 mins then place everything to the side.

- Now stir fry your chicken in the bacon grease for about 7 mins per side until fully done.
- Now place the chicken to the side with the bacon.
- Now turn on your broiler and ensure that the rack is at least 6 inches from the heating source.
- Add to the bacon fat, the following: brown sugar, onions, pepper flakes, lemon pepper, salt, Italian seasoning.
- Stir fry for 13 mins.
- Put your chicken in a broiler pan or cookie sheet and add to 2 pieces of bacon to each and then some onion mix and Monterey.
- Cook everything in the broiler for 2 to 4 mins to melt the cheese.
- Enjoy.

Amount per serving (4 total)

Timing Information:

Preparation	10 m
Cooking	35 m
Total Time	45 m

Nutritional Information:

Calories	664 kcal
Fat	35.7 g
Carbohydrates	34.5g
Protein	48.7 g
Cholesterol	152 mg
Sodium	1823 mg

* Percent Daily Values are based on a 2,000 calorie diet.

LEMON LIME SODA CHICKEN

Ingredients

- 1 1/2 C. lemon-lime soda
- 1/2 C. olive oil
- 1/2 C. soy sauce
- 1/4 tsp garlic powder
- 4 (6 oz.) skinless, boneless chicken breast halves

Directions

- Get a bowl, combine: garlic powder, lemon soda, soy sauce, and olive oil.
- Combine in your chicken and place in everything the fridge for 8 hrs.
- Now heat up your grill and get the grate coated with oil.
- For 8 mins on each side grill your chicken.
- Let them cool off before serving.
- Enjoy.

Amount per serving (4 total)

Timing Information:

Preparation	5 m
Cooking	15 m
Total Time	8 h 20 m

Nutritional Information:

Calories	488 kcal
Fat	31.6 g
Carbohydrates	12.7g
Protein	37.4 g
Cholesterol	97 mg
Sodium	1899 mg

* Percent Daily Values are based on a 2,000 calorie diet.

Easy Japanese Style Chicken Breast

Ingredients

- 1 lb boneless skinless chicken breasts
- 1 egg
- 1 C. panko crumbs
- 1/2 tsp Sea Salt
- 1/4 tsp Black Pepper
- 1/2 tsp Garlic Powder
- 1/2 tsp Onion Powder
- 1/4 C. Corn Oil

Directions

- With a mallet, flatten your chicken, and then dip them in whisked egg, and a mix of: onion powder, salt, garlic powder, panko, and pepper.
- For 4 mins on each side cook your chicken in hot oil until fully done.
- Drain off excess oils with some paper towel.
- Enjoy.

Amount per serving (4 total)

Timing Information:

Preparation	10 m
Cooking	4 m
Total Time	14 m

Nutritional Information:

Calories	335 kcal
Fat	17.5 g
Carbohydrates	19.6g
Protein	30.8 g
Cholesterol	112 mg
Sodium	546 mg

* Percent Daily Values are based on a 2,000 calorie diet.

TOMATOES AND ONION CHICKEN

Ingredients

- 1 (32 fluid oz.) container chicken stock
- 32 fluid oz. water, or more if needed
- 1 yellow onion, peeled and slits cut into it
- 1 bunch celery, stalks (including leaves) separated
- 3 carrots
- 2 tbsps tomato paste, or more to taste
- 1 tbsp salt
- 5 whole black peppercorns
- 1 bay leaf
- 2 lbs skinless, boneless chicken breast halves, each cut in half

Directions

- Get the following boiling: bay leaf, stock, peppercorns, water, salt, onions, tomato paste, carrots, and celery.
- Once everything is boiling set the heat to low and let it gently cook for 40 mins.
- Add in your chicken and make sure ii is fully submerged if not, add some water.

- Get everything boiling again for about 2 mins then add a tight lid on the pot and shut the heat.
- Let the chicken poach for 20 mins until fully done.
- Check the internal temperature of the chicken it should be 165 degrees.
- Enjoy.

Amount per serving (4 total)

Timing Information:

Preparation	15 m
Cooking	45 m
Total Time	1 h

Nutritional Information:

Calories	322 kcal
Fat	3.9 g
Carbohydrates	14.4g
Protein	55.2 g
Cholesterol	1133 mg
Sodium	2786 mg

* Percent Daily Values are based on a 2,000 calorie diet.

Rustic Style Chicken

Ingredients

- 1/4 C. unsalted butter
- 2 bone-in skin-on chicken breasts
- 4 potatoes, peeled and cut into 1-inch cubes
- 4 carrots, peeled and cut into 1/2-inch rounds
- 3 stalks celery, cut into 1/2-inch slices
- 1 tbsp fresh rosemary
- 1 tsp fresh lemon thyme leaves
- 1/2 tsp smoked paprika
- 1/2 tsp garlic powder
- 1/2 tsp seasoned salt
- 1/4 tsp ground white pepper
- salt and ground black pepper to taste

Directions

- Get your thyme and rosemary and chop it nicely then place it to the side in a bowl. Then also add to the spice: black pepper, paprika, salt, garlic powder, white pepper, and season salt.
- Cook your chicken in butter for 6 mins then turn over the chicken and place the following veggies around the chicken: celery, potatoes, and carrots.

- Top everything with the thyme spice mix and put a lid on the pot. Cook for 47 mins with a medium to low level of heat.
- Ensure the internal temp of the chicken is 165 before serving.
- Enjoy.

Amount per serving (4 total)

Timing Information:

Preparation	15 m
Cooking	50 m
Total Time	1 h 5 m

Nutritional Information:

Calories	601 kcal
Fat	23.7 g
Carbohydrates	45.8g
Protein	50.4 g
Cholesterol	1157 mg
Sodium	407 mg

* Percent Daily Values are based on a 2,000 calorie diet.

SAVORY GARLIC CHICKEN BREAST

Ingredients

- cooking spray
- 1 clove garlic, minced
- 4 skinless, boneless chicken breast halves
- salt and ground black pepper to taste
- 3/4 C. chicken broth
- 1 tbsp lemon juice

Directions

- Stir fry your garlic, for 5 mins, in a pan with nonstick spray.
- Then add in your chicken after coating it with some pepper and salt and cook for 14 mins.
- Pour in your lemon juice and broth and get everything boiling.
- Once everything is boiling, place a lid on the pot, set the heat to low, and let the chicken gently cook for 17 mins.
- Place your chicken to the side and continue gently cooking your broth mix for about 4 more mins until it has reduced. Then top your chicken with it.
- Enjoy.

Amount per serving (4 total)

Timing Information:

Preparation	10 m
Cooking	25 m
Total Time	35 m

Nutritional Information:

Calories	131 kcal
Fat	2.9 g
Carbohydrates	0.8g
Protein	23.8 g
Cholesterol	66 mg
Sodium	275 mg

* Percent Daily Values are based on a 2,000 calorie diet.

Teriyaki, Tomatillos, and Muenster Chicken

Ingredients

- 1 (12 fluid oz.) can or bottle beer
- 1/2 C. teriyaki sauce
- 1 tbsp chili powder
- 1 tsp garlic powder
- 8 skinless, boneless chicken breast halves
- 8 slices Muenster cheese
- 3 1/2 lbs fresh tomatillos, husks removed
- 1/2 C. water
- 1 onion, chopped
- 6 cloves garlic, chopped, or more to taste
- 1 pinch salt and ground black pepper to taste
- 1/4 C. chopped fresh cilantro
- 1 C. sour cream

Directions

- Get a bowl, combine: garlic powder, beer, chili powder, and teriyaki. Add in your chicken and place a covering on the bowl, let the chicken marinate overnight.
- Now heat up your grill and get the grate ready by coating it with some oil.

- For 8 mins per side grill your chicken. Then place the cooked chicken in a casserole dish and add a topping of Muenster.
- Now set your oven to 350 degrees before doing anything else.
- Get the following boiling: water and tomatillos.
- Once everything is boiling, place a lid on the pan, set the heat to low, and cook the mix for 11 mins.
- Add in the garlic and onions and also some pepper and salt and gently cook for 17 mins.
- Puree this sauce in a food processor or blender and then once it is smooth add in cilantro and sour cream.
- Blend the mix again and then top your chicken with this sauce.
- Cook everything in the oven for 17 mins.
- Enjoy.

Amount per serving (8 total)

Timing Information:

Preparation	20 m
Cooking	30 m
Total Time	6 h 50 m

Nutritional Information:

Calories	399 kcal
Fat	19.1 g
Carbohydrates	21.8g
Protein	33.4 g
Cholesterol	98 mg
Sodium	948 mg

* Percent Daily Values are based on a 2,000 calorie diet.

CHICKEN BREAST DUMP DINNER

Ingredients

- 1 lb skinless, boneless chicken breast halves
- 1 (14.5 oz.) can petite diced tomatoes
- 1/4 onion, chopped (optional)
- 1 tsp Italian seasoning (optional)
- 1 clove garlic, minced (optional)

Directions

- Add your chicken to a crock pot and then pour in: garlic, tomatoes, Italian seasoning, and onions.
- Let this cook in the slow cooker for 8 hrs. with a low level of heat.
- Let the contents cool for about 10 mins uncovered and then add in your preferred amount of pepper and salt.
- Enjoy with cooked Jasmin rice.

Amount per serving (4 total)

Timing Information:

Preparation	10 m
Cooking	6 h
Total Time	6 h 10 m

Nutritional Information:

Calories	144 kcal
Fat	2.4 g
Carbohydrates	5.2g
Protein	23.1 g
Cholesterol	59 mg
Sodium	208 mg

* Percent Daily Values are based on a 2,000 calorie diet.

Mozzarella, Rosemary, and Marsala Chicken

Ingredients

- 8 skinless, boneless chicken breast halves
- 1/2 C. all-purpose flour
- 1 tsp poultry seasoning
- 1 tbsp butter
- 1 tbsp olive oil
- 1/4 C. Marsala wine
- 1 C. chopped Portobello mushrooms
- 1 C. chopped onion
- 1 tsp dried rosemary
- 4 slices mozzarella cheese

Directions

- Coat your chicken with a mix of poultry seasoning and flour. Then for 6 mins on each side fry each piece of chicken in butter and then set it to the side.
- Add in your wine and scrape up any browned bits in the pan and then combine in: rosemary, mushrooms, and onions.
- Stir fry everything for 7 mins and then add in your chicken back to the pan.

- Coat your chicken with the sauce and then add a topping of cheese on each.
- Cook the contents for 3 mins with a lid and then shut the heat and let it sit for 12 mins.
- Ensure that your chicken is fully done before serving.
- Enjoy.

Amount per serving (4 total)

Timing Information:

Preparation	10 m
Cooking	50 m
Total Time	1 h

Nutritional Information:

Calories	492 kcal
Fat	13.9 g
Carbohydrates	20.1g
Protein	64 g
Cholesterol	1162 mg
Sodium	352 mg

* Percent Daily Values are based on a 2,000 calorie diet.

Buttery Mushrooms and Cheese Chicken

Ingredients

- 6 skinless, boneless chicken breast halves
- salt and pepper to taste
- 1 pinch paprika, or to taste
- 3 tbsps butter
- 1 (10.75 oz.) can condensed cream of mushroom soup
- 1/3 C. milk
- 2 tbsps minced onion
- 1/2 C. processed cheese (such as Velveeta(R)), diced
- 2 tbsps Worcestershire sauce
- 1 (4.5 oz.) can sliced mushrooms, drained and chopped
- 2/3 C. sour cream

Directions

- Coat a baking dish with oil or nonstick spray and then set your oven to 350 degrees before doing anything else.
- Coat your chicken pieces with: paprika, salt, and pepper and then fry them in butter for 6 mins per side.
- Place all the chicken in the dish.

- Now get a big pot and heat the following but do not boil it: mushrooms, mushroom soup, Worcestershire, milk, cheese, and onions.
- You want to continue heating until everything is hot and the cheese is melted and combined with the mix.
- Top your chicken with this sauce and cook everything in the oven for 46 mins then baste the chicken and cook for 30 more mins.
- Enjoy.

NOTE: If you like you can baste the chicken more than once but at least once is recommended.

Amount per serving (6 total)

Timing Information:

Preparation	25 m
Cooking	1 h 35 m
Total Time	2 h

Nutritional Information:

Calories	335 kcal
Fat	20.6 g
Carbohydrates	8.9g
Protein	28.2 g
Cholesterol	100 mg
Sodium	769 mg

* Percent Daily Values are based on a 2,000 calorie diet.

BITE SIZED BAKE CHICKEN

Ingredients

- 1 lb skinless, boneless chicken breast halves - cut into bite size pieces
- 4 tbsps butter, melted
- 1 1/4 C. Italian seasoned bread crumbs

Directions

- Set your oven to 325 degrees before doing anything else.
- Get your margarine melted in a bowl and coat your chicken in it.
- Now dip the coated chicken in breadcrumbs.
- Cook the chicken in the oven for 12 mins then flip them and cook for 8 to 10 more mins.
- Enjoy.

Amount per serving (4 total)

Timing Information:

Preparation	10 m
Cooking	30 m
Total Time	50 m

Nutritional Information:

Calories	371 kcal
Fat	16.3 g
Carbohydrates	25.7g
Protein	29 g
Cholesterol	96 mg
Sodium	798 mg

* Percent Daily Values are based on a 2,000 calorie diet.

CARROTS, PEPPERS, AND PARSLEY CHICKEN BREAST

Ingredients

- 4 skinless, boneless chicken breast halves
- 8 carrots, sliced into 1/2-inch rounds
- 4 green bell peppers, sliced
- 8 stalks celery, chopped
- 8 green onions, chopped
- 1/4 C. chopped fresh flat-leaf parsley
- 1/2 C. olive oil
- 1 tsp salt
- 1 tsp Italian seasoning
- 1 tsp chili powder
- 1 tsp lemon pepper
- 4 pinches freshly ground black pepper, or to taste

Directions

- Set your oven to 375 degrees before doing anything else.
- Layer your chicken in a casserole dish then surround it with: parsley, carrots, onions, bell peppers, and celery.
- Cover everything with: black and lemon pepper, salt, chili powder, and Italian seasoning.
- Cook the dish in the oven for 35 mins. Enjoy.

Amount per serving (4 total)

Timing Information:

Preparation	20 m
Cooking	30 m
Total Time	50 m

Nutritional Information:

Calories	485 kcal
Fat	31.5 g
Carbohydrates	23.8g
Protein	29 g
Cholesterol	69 mg
Sodium	923 mg

* Percent Daily Values are based on a 2,000 calorie diet.

PINEAPPLE, LIME, AND GARLIC CHICKEN BREAST

Ingredients

- 1/4 C. olive oil
- 1/4 C. lime juice
- 1 tbsp minced garlic
- 1/2 C. of pineapple, no juice
- salt and ground black pepper to taste
- 2 skinless, boneless chicken breast halves

Directions

- Marinate your chicken in a mix of: black pepper, olive oil, salt, garlic, and lime juice. Let it sit overnight.
- Set your oven to 400 degrees before doing anything else.
- Place your chicken in a casserole dish and then top it with more black pepper and salt before cooking everything in the oven for 35 mins.
- When five mins is left in the cooking time top your chicken with the pineapple chunks.
- Then continue baking. Enjoy.

Amount per serving (2 total)

Timing Information:

Preparation	10 m
Cooking	25 m
Total Time	3 h 35 m

Nutritional Information:

Calories	378 kcal
Fat	29.8 g
Carbohydrates	4g
Protein	24 g
Cholesterol	65 mg
Sodium	58 mg

* Percent Daily Values are based on a 2,000 calorie diet.

PARMESAN, SPINACH, AND PESTO CHICKEN

Ingredients

- 1 1/2 C. finely chopped fresh spinach
- 2 tbsps basil pesto, or to taste
- 4 skinless, boneless chicken breast halves
- 2 tbsps grated Parmesan cheese (optional)

Directions

- Set your oven to 375 degrees before doing anything else.
- Get a bowl, combine: pesto and spinach.
- Layer half of the mix in a casserole dish then layer your chicken pieces and top everything with the rest of the mix.
- Place some foil around the casserole dish and cook in the contents in the oven for 35 mins.
- Add your preferred amount of pepper and salt. Then top the chicken with your parmesan.
- Cook everything for 17 more mins in the oven.
- Enjoy.

Amount per serving (4 total)

Timing Information:

Preparation	10 m
Cooking	45 m
Total Time	55 m

Nutritional Information:

Calories	179 kcal
Fat	7.1 g
Carbohydrates	1.3g
Protein	26.5 g
Cholesterol	69 mg
Sodium	169 mg

* Percent Daily Values are based on a 2,000 calorie diet.

Easy BBQ Style Chicken (Grilled)

Ingredients

- 2 skinless, boneless chicken breasts
- 1 C. Italian-style salad dressing
- 1 (18 oz.) bottle barbecue sauce

Directions

- Get a bowl and combine in it your frozen chicken and dressing.
- Place a covering over the bowl and then place it in the fridge until the chicken is no longer frozen.
- Now get your grill hot and get the grate ready by coating it with oil.
- For 7 mins per side cook your chicken on the grill.
- Flip the chicken pieces and then coat them with bbq sauce liberally.
- Enjoy.

Amount per serving (2 total)

Timing Information:

Preparation	2 h
Cooking	20 m
Total Time	2 h 30 m

Nutritional Information:

Calories	850 kcal
Fat	35.5 g
Carbohydrates	103.6g
Protein	27.7 g
Cholesterol	68 mg
Sodium	4840 mg

* Percent Daily Values are based on a 2,000 calorie diet.

Stuffed Chicken Breast IV
(Crawfish, Crab, and Mushrooms)

Ingredients

- 8 skinless, boneless chicken breast halves
- 1 C. Worcestershire sauce
- 2 C. unsalted butter
- 1 C. diced onion
- 1 C. diced celery
- 1/2 C. diced green bell pepper
- 3 tbsps minced garlic
- 1 lb cooked and peeled crawfish tails, coarsely chopped
- salt
- black pepper
- 1 C. all-purpose flour
- 1 pint heavy whipping cream
- 12 oz. fresh oyster mushrooms, stemmed and sliced
- 2 C. fresh lump crabmeat
- 1 C. diced green onion

Directions

- With a mallet flatten your chicken on a working surface then put them in a bowl, with the Worcestershire sauce.
- Place everything in the fridge.

- Meanwhile stir fry your garlic, onions, bell peppers, and celery in butter (half a C.) for 17 mins then combine in the fish and cook for 7 more mins.
- Now add in the pepper and salt.
- Place everything to the side in a big bowl.
- Coat your chicken with some flour and then brown it in butter (half a C.).
- Set your oven to 375 degrees before doing anything else.
- Lay your chicken flat and add an equal amount of crawfish mix to it. Then fold it up and stake a toothpick through it. Place everything in a casserole dish.
- For 7 mins cook the following: green onions, cream, mushrooms, and butter (1 C.).
- Top your chicken wraps with the cream mix and an equal amount of crabmeat.
- Place a wrapping of foil around the entire dish and cook everything in the oven for 50 mins.
- Enjoy.

Amount per serving (8 total)

Timing Information:

Preparation	1 h
Cooking	1 h
Total Time	2 h

Nutritional Information:

Calories	1073 kcal
Fat	72.5 g
Carbohydrates	128.2g
Protein	75.8 g
Cholesterol	1437 mg
Sodium	1715 mg

* Percent Daily Values are based on a 2,000 calorie diet.

Coconut Cooked Chicken Breast (Paleo Approved)

Ingredients

- 3/4 C. coconut milk
- 1 egg
- 6 oz. unsweetened flaked coconut, or more as needed
- 2 lbs skinless, boneless chicken breast halves
- 1/4 C. butter

Directions

- Get a bowl, combine: eggs, and coconut milk.
- Get a 2nd bowl for your coconut flakes.
- With a mallet flatten out your chicken on a working surface.
- Coat the chicken with the egg mix and then the flakes. Layer the chicken in a big dish so as to avoid stacking.
- Fry each piece in butter for 8 mins each side.
- Enjoy.

Amount per serving (4 total)

Timing Information:

Preparation	10 m
Cooking	15 m
Total Time	25 m

Nutritional Information:

Calories	768 kcal
Fat	56.4 g
Carbohydrates	12.1g
Protein	56.3 g
Cholesterol	1215 mg
Sodium	241 mg

* Percent Daily Values are based on a 2,000 calorie diet.

HONEY MUSTARD, AND MUSHROOM CHICKEN

Ingredients

- 1/8 C. Italian-style dried bread crumbs
- 4 skinless, boneless chicken breasts
- 1 tbsp olive oil
- 1/2 C. dry white wine
- 1/2 tsp ground savory
- 1/4 tsp salt
- 1 (4.5 oz.) can sliced mushrooms
- 1 tbsp lemon juice
- 1 tbsp honey mustard

Directions

- Coat your chicken pieces with breadcrumbs and then cook each for 4 mins per side.
- Then add in with the chicken: mushrooms, wine, salt, and savory.
- Get the contents boiling, place a lid on the pot, set the heat to low, and gently cook for 17 mins.
- Take out your chicken and place it to the side.
- Add in the mustard and lemon juice to the pot and get it hot for 2 mins.
- Top the chicken with the lemon mix. Enjoy.

Amount per serving (4 total)

Timing Information:

Preparation	10 m
Cooking	50 m
Total Time	1 h 20 m

Nutritional Information:

Calories	217 kcal
Fat	5.4 g
Carbohydrates	7.2g
Protein	28.6 g
Cholesterol	69 mg
Sodium	454 mg

* Percent Daily Values are based on a 2,000 calorie diet.

RED PEPPER, CILANTRO, AND LIME CHICKEN BREAST

Ingredients

- 1/2 C. orange juice
- 1/2 lime, juiced
- 1 tbsp honey
- 1 tsp crushed red pepper flakes
- 4 (6 oz.) skinless, boneless chicken breast halves
- 1 tbsp chopped fresh cilantro

Directions

- Get a bowl, combine: pepper flakes, orange juice, honey, and lime juice.
- Place your chicken in the mix and stir everything before placing a covering on the bowl and letting it marinate in the fridge for 40 mins.
- Get your grill hot and get the grate ready by applying some oil to it.
- Grill the chicken for 7 mins then flip it and cook for 7 more mins.
- Before serving the chicken add a garnishing of cilantro.
- Enjoy.

Amount per serving (4 total)

Timing Information:

Preparation	5 m
Cooking	12 m
Total Time	47 m

Nutritional Information:

Calories	223 kcal
Fat	4.3 g
Carbohydrates	8.9g
Protein	35.8 g
Cholesterol	97 mg
Sodium	86 mg

* Percent Daily Values are based on a 2,000 calorie diet.

STUFFED CHICKEN BREAST V
(CRAB, CREAM CHEESE, AND GARLIC)

Ingredients

- 3 oz. cream cheese, softened
- 2 tbsps minced onion
- 2 tbsps chopped fresh parsley
- 1 tsp chopped fresh dill
- 1 tsp minced garlic
- 1/8 tsp lemon pepper
- 4 oz. fresh Dungeness crabmeat
- 4 skinless, boneless chicken breasts
- 1 C. all-purpose flour
- 2 eggs, beaten
- 3 C. fresh bread crumbs
- 2 tbsps butter
- 2 tbsps vegetable oil

Directions

- Get a bowl, mix: lemon pepper, cream cheese, black pepper, crab, garlic, onions, salt, dill, and parsley.
- Place a covering on the bowl, and then enter it into the fridge for 20 mins or until cold.
- Slice an opening into your chicken pieces by cutting a slit through them horizontally.

- Then stuff the chicken pieces with an equal amount of filling. Coat your chicken with whisked egg and then a mix of bread crumbs and flour.
- For 11 mins per side fry the chicken in butter then place them on some paper towel to remove the oil excess.
- Enjoy.

Amount per serving (4 total)

Timing Information:

Preparation	10 m
Cooking	30 m
Total Time	1 h

Nutritional Information:

Calories	569 kcal
Fat	25.4 g
Carbohydrates	41.9g
Protein	42.7 g
Cholesterol	217 mg
Sodium	544 mg

* Percent Daily Values are based on a 2,000 calorie diet.

Stuffed Chicken Breast VI

(Bacon, Cornbread, and Jam)

Ingredients

- 1 tbsp olive oil
- 2 (6 oz.) skinless, boneless chicken breast halves
- Salt and pepper to taste
- 2 pieces cornbread, crumbled
- 2 slices cooked turkey bacon, crumbled
- 2 tbsps minced celery
- 2 tbsps minced onion
- 2 tbsps butter, melted
- 1/4 C. chicken stock
- 1/3 C. chicken stock
- 1/3 C. plum jam

Directions

- Set your oven to 350 degrees before doing anything else.
- Cut an opening in your chicken pieces before searing them in olive oil. Place them to the side.
- Get a bowl, mix: 1/4 C. chicken stock, cornbread, butter, bacon, onions, and celery. Fill each piece of chicken with this mix.
- Cook the chicken, in a casserole dish, in the oven for 30 mins.

- At the same time get 1/3 a C. of stock boiling then add in jam and gently cook with a low heat until the stock has cooked out.
- Halfway through the cooking time of the chicken, top it with the plum sauce and continue cooking in the oven.
- Enjoy.

Amount per serving (2 total)

Timing Information:

Preparation	15 m
Cooking	40 m
Total Time	55 m

Nutritional Information:

Calories	684 kcal
Fat	30 g
Carbohydrates	61.1g
Protein	42.1 g
Cholesterol	156 mg
Sodium	867 mg

* Percent Daily Values are based on a 2,000 calorie diet.

Tarragon, Olives, and Lemon Chicken

Ingredients

- 2 tbsps butter
- 2 tbsps minced garlic
- 1 large lemon, juiced
- 1/2 tsp dried tarragon
- 4 boneless, skinless chicken breasts
- 20 pitted green olives

Directions

- Set your oven to 350 degrees before doing anything else.
- Stir fry: tarragon, garlic, and lemon juice in butter for 1 min.
- Then add in your chicken and cook for 6 mins each side.
- Pour in the olives and cook for 1 more min before entering the pan into the oven for 25 mins.
- Enjoy.

Amount per serving (4 total)

Timing Information:

Preparation	10 m
Cooking	30 m
Total Time	40 m

Nutritional Information:

Calories	216 kcal
Fat	11.2 g
Carbohydrates	4.7g
Protein	25.5 g
Cholesterol	82 mg
Sodium	569 mg

* Percent Daily Values are based on a 2,000 calorie diet.

Stuffed Chicken Breast VII

(Peppers, Onions, Squash, and Cheddar)

Ingredients

- 1 tbsp butter
- 1/2 C. finely diced acorn squash
- 1 green bell pepper, diced
- 1 small onion, finely diced
- 1 stalk celery, chopped
- salt and pepper to taste
- 4 skinless, boneless chicken breasts
- 2 oz. shredded Cheddar cheese
- 2 C. all-purpose flour for coating

Directions

- Coat a casserole dish with nonstick spray or oil and then set your oven to 350 degrees before doing anything else.
- Stir fry your celery, squash, onions, and bell peppers in butter until soft then add in some pepper and salt.

- Shut the heat and add in the cheese.
- Stir the mix a bit.
- Cut an opening into your chicken pieces and add an equal amount of mix to each. Coat the chicken with flour and sear it in a pan with some oil.
- After searing the chicken pieces.
- Layer them in the casserole dish and cook for 35 mins in the oven.
- Enjoy.

Amount per serving (4 total)

Timing Information:

Preparation	10 m
Cooking	1 h
Total Time	1 h 20 m

Nutritional Information:

Calories	461 kcal
Fat	9.8 g
Carbohydrates	53g
Protein	37.9 g
Cholesterol	91 mg
Sodium	197 mg

* Percent Daily Values are based on a 2,000 calorie diet.

Easy Artisan Style Chicken

Ingredients

- 1 tbsp olive oil
- 3 skinless, boneless chicken breast halves
- 1 tbsp ground black pepper, or to taste
- 3 tbsps onion powder, or to taste
- 1 (28 oz.) can chopped stewed tomatoes, 1/2 the liquid reserved
- 1 (14 oz.) can chicken broth
- 1 (10 oz.) package frozen mixed vegetables
- 1/4 C. water

Directions

- Coat your chicken with some onion power and pepper before cooking for 3 mins per side in oil.
- Add in the tomatoes with juice and the broth.
- Get everything boiling, then place a lid on the pot, set the heat to low, and let the contents cook for 17 mins on each side.
- At the same time get your veggies boiling in water.
- Once everything is boiling add about 3/4 of a C. of tomato mix to the veggies and cook for 7 more mins.

- Remove all the liquid and then serve the veggies with chicken on top.
- Liberally top the chicken and veggies with more tomato sauce.
- Enjoy.

Amount per serving (3 total)

Timing Information:

Preparation	10 m
Cooking	35 m
Total Time	45 m

Nutritional Information:

Calories	325 kcal
Fat	8.3 g
Carbohydrates	36.2g
Protein	30 g
Cholesterol	64 mg
Sodium	1302 mg

* Percent Daily Values are based on a 2,000 calorie diet.

Nutmeg, Almonds, and Mushroom Chicken

Ingredients

- 4 skinless, boneless chicken breast halves
- salt and pepper to taste
- 1 egg
- 1/2 C. water
- 2 C. finely chopped almonds
- 1/4 C. butter
- 3 tbsps olive oil
- 1 lb fresh mushrooms
- 1 onion, sliced into rings
- 2 cloves garlic, crushed
- 1 C. heavy cream
- 1/4 C. almond paste
- 1/2 tsp freshly ground nutmeg

Directions

- With a mallet flatten your chicken and then top everything with some pepper and salt.
- Now set your oven to 350 degrees before doing anything else.
- Get a bowl, and combine in: water and eggs.
- Get a 2nd bowl for the almond crumbs.
- Dip your chicken in the eggs first and then crumbs then sear each piece in butter.

- Place everything in a casserole dish.
- Stir fry your onions, garlic, and mushrooms for 5 mins then top your chicken with it.
- In the same pan combine the almond paste and cream and get it hot but not boiling then add the nutmeg and then pour it over the chicken as well.
- Cook everything in the oven for 45 mins.
- Enjoy.

Amount per serving (4 total)

Timing Information:

Preparation	20 m
Cooking	40 m
Total Time	1 h

Nutritional Information:

Calories	1095 kcal
Fat	88.8 g
Carbohydrates	133.1g
Protein	52.1 g
Cholesterol	1227 mg
Sodium	206 mg

* Percent Daily Values are based on a 2,000 calorie diet.

Sweet Potatoes and Balsamic Bake

Ingredients

- 2 sweet potatoes, peeled and cut into 2-inch pieces
- 1 tbsp olive oil
- salt and pepper to taste
- 2 skinless, boneless chicken breast halves
- 1/2 C. balsamic vinegar
- salt and ground black pepper to taste
- 1/2 C. balsamic vinegar

Directions

- Set your oven to 400 degrees before doing anything else.
- Get a bowl, combine: potatoes, olive oil, pepper and salt.
- Once everything is evenly coated place them in a baking dish and cook everything in the oven for 30 mins.
- Coat your chicken with pepper and salt and then layer them in another casserole dish. Top the chicken with half a C. of balsamic.
- Wrap foil around the dish and cook everything in the oven for 20 mins.
- Turn your potatoes and chicken over and then cook for 20 more mins with a 350 degree level of heat.

- Meanwhile boil the remaining balsamic (half a C.) until half of it has evaporated.
- When the chicken and potatoes are done top them with the balsamic before serving.
- Enjoy.

Amount per serving (2 total)

Timing Information:

Preparation	10 m
Cooking	50 m
Total Time	1 h

Nutritional Information:

Calories	379 kcal
Fat	8.5 g
Carbohydrates	44.7g
Protein	29.8 g
Cholesterol	68 mg
Sodium	179 mg

* Percent Daily Values are based on a 2,000 calorie diet.

CREAMY RASPBERRIES AND SHALLOTS CHICKEN

Ingredients

- 2 skinless, boneless chicken breasts
- 2 tbsps butter
- 1 tbsp vegetable oil
- 3 tbsps shallots, minced
- 1/3 C. chicken stock
- 1/4 C. raspberry vinegar
- 1/3 C. heavy whipping cream
- salt and pepper to taste

Directions

- Fry your chicken in a big pot in butter until fully done then place them to the side.
- In the same pan add: chicken stock, and shallots.
- Cook for 5 mins then add the vinegar and get everything boiling.
- Boil and stir until you find that the stock has become a bit thicker and then add the cream and the chicken.

- Cook for 3 mins then add some pepper and salt.
- Enjoy.

Amount per serving (4 total)

Timing Information:

Preparation	10 m
Cooking	30 m
Total Time	1 h

Nutritional Information:

Calories	229 kcal
Fat	17.3 g
Carbohydrates	4g
Protein	14.3 g
Cholesterol	77 mg
Sodium	91 mg

* Percent Daily Values are based on a 2,000 calorie diet.

LIME AND CHIVES CHICKEN BREAST

Ingredients

- 4 skinless, boneless chicken breast halves - flattened
- 1 egg, beaten
- 2/3 C. dry bread crumbs
- 2 tbsps olive oil
- 1 lime, juiced
- 6 tbsps butter
- 1 tsp minced fresh chives
- 1/2 tsp dried dill weed

Directions

- Get a bowl for your eggs.
- Get a 2nd bowl for your bread crumbs.
- Dip your chicken pieces first in eggs and then in the crumbs.
- Now place them on a wire rack, in the open, for 15 mins, to dry out.
- For 6 mins on each side fry your chicken in olive oil then place them to the side.
- Remove any excess oils then add the butter and lime juice.

- Heat and stir for a few mins until the butter is fully melted than add the dill and chives.
- Top the chicken with the lime juice and serve.
- Enjoy.

Amount per serving (4 total)

Timing Information:

Preparation	15 m
Cooking	15 m
Total Time	30 m

Nutritional Information:

Calories	455 kcal
Fat	30 g
Carbohydrates	15.3g
Protein	30.7 g
Cholesterol	164 mg
Sodium	335 mg

* Percent Daily Values are based on a 2,000 calorie diet.

MAPLE SYRUP AND PECANS CHICKEN BREAST

Ingredients

- 4 skinless, boneless chicken breasts
- 2 tbsps real maple syrup
- 1 C. chopped pecans
- 3 tbsps all-purpose flour
- 1 tsp salt
- 2 tbsps butter
- 1 tbsp vegetable oil

Directions

- Get a bowl, combine: salt, flour, and pecans.
- Coat your chicken pieces with syrup then cover each piece with the pecans.
- Fry these chicken pieces in butter for 14 mins.
- Enjoy with some cooked brown rice.

Amount per serving (4 total)

Timing Information:

Preparation	10 m
Cooking	15 m
Total Time	25 m

Nutritional Information:

Calories	447 kcal
Fat	30.3 g
Carbohydrates	15g
Protein	30.4 g
Cholesterol	84 mg
Sodium	700 mg

* Percent Daily Values are based on a 2,000 calorie diet.

Easy Backroad Style Chicken

Ingredients

- 4 skinless, boneless chicken breast halves
- 1 C. Worcestershire sauce
- 1 C. vegetable oil
- 1 C. lemon juice
- 1 tsp garlic powder

Directions

- Get a bowl, combine: garlic, Worcestershire, lemon juice, and oil. Place a lid on the bowl, and marinate everything in the fridge overnight.
- Turn on your oven's broiler and ensure that the grate is 6 inches away from the heating source.
- Once the broiler is hot, broil your chicken for 8 mins per side until cooked fully.
- Enjoy.

Amount per serving (4 total)

Timing Information:

Preparation	10 m
Cooking	20 m
Total Time	8 h 30 m

Nutritional Information:

Calories	676 kcal
Fat	57.4 g
Carbohydrates	19g
Protein	23.3 g
Cholesterol	61 mg
Sodium	717 mg

* Percent Daily Values are based on a 2,000 calorie diet.

Stuffed Chicken Breast VIII (Apples and Cheddar)

Ingredients

- 2 skinless, boneless chicken breasts
- 1/2 C. chopped apple
- 2 tbsps shredded Cheddar cheese
- 1 tbsp Italian-style dried bread crumbs
- 1 tbsp butter
- 1/4 C. dry white wine
- 1/4 C. water
- 1 tbsp water
- 1 1/2 tsps cornstarch
- 1 tbsp chopped fresh parsley, for garnish

Directions

- Get a bowl, mix: bread crumbs, cheese, and apples.
- With a mallet pound out your chicken pieces, then add an equal amount of filling to the center of each.

- Shape the chicken pieces into a roll and then stake a toothpick through each.
- Sear your chicken in butter then once it is browned all over add your water and wine.
- Place a lid on the pan and let the contents gently cook for 17 mins.
- Place your chicken on a serving platter and then add some cornstarch and a tbsp of water to the remaining wine in the pot.
- Heat and stir the cornstarch to form a gravy to top your chicken with.
- Serve the chicken rolls with a topping of parsley and gravy.
- Enjoy.

Amount per serving (4 total)

Timing Information:

Preparation	15 m
Cooking	25 m
Total Time	40 m

Nutritional Information:

Calories	139 kcal
Fat	5.1 g
Carbohydrates	4.9g
Protein	15 g
Cholesterol	46 mg
Sodium	120 mg

* Percent Daily Values are based on a 2,000 calorie diet.

Buttery Capers and Lemon Chicken

Ingredients

- 4 boneless, skinless chicken breast halves
- 1 tsp lemon pepper
- 1 tsp salt
- 1 tsp dried dill weed
- 1 tsp garlic powder
- 3 tbsps butter
- 1/2 C. whipping cream
- 2 tbsps capers, drained and rinsed

Directions

- Coat your chicken with garlic powder, lemon pepper, dill, and salt. Then for 6 mins sear the chicken in butter making sure to turn the chicken repeatedly.
- Set your heat to low and cook the contents for 8 mins until fully done.
- Place your chicken to the side and wrap them with some foil.
- In the same pan turn up the heat and add in whipping cream.
- Cook the cream for 4 mins while stirring then add the capers.

- Top the chicken with the cream and serve with some cooked angel hair pasta.
- Enjoy.

Amount per serving (4 total)

Timing Information:

Preparation	5 m
Cooking	15 m
Total Time	20 m

Nutritional Information:

Calories	313 kcal
Fat	21.2 g
Carbohydrates	1.8g
Protein	28.2 g
Cholesterol	132 mg
Sodium	974 mg

* Percent Daily Values are based on a 2,000 calorie diet.

BUTTERMILK AND HONEY CHICKEN

Ingredients

- 3 C. cold water
- 1/4 C. kosher salt
- 1/4 C. honey
- 4 boneless skinless chicken breast halves
- 1/4 C. buttermilk
- 1 C. all-purpose flour
- 1 tsp black pepper
- 1/2 tsp garlic salt
- 1/2 tsp onion salt
- cayenne pepper to taste
- vegetable oil for frying

Directions

- Get a bowl, combine: honey, water, and salt.
- Stir the mix for a few mins then add in your chicken and place everything in the fridge for 60 mins covered.
- Then drain the liquid.
- Add in your buttermilk and let the chicken sit in the milk for 20 mins.

- Get a 2nd bowl, add: cayenne, flour, onion salt, black pepper, and garlic salt.
- Dredge the chicken in the flour and then place them in on a wire rack for 20 mins.
- Get your veggie oil hot then fry the chicken in it for 16 mins. Ensure that the internal temperature of the chicken is 165 before serving.
- Let the chicken cool for 10 mins.
- Enjoy.

Amount per serving (4 total)

Timing Information:

Preparation	10 m
Cooking	15 m
Total Time	1 h 45 m

Nutritional Information:

Calories	481 kcal
Fat	21.5 g
Carbohydrates	49.4g
Protein	22.8 g
Cholesterol	65 mg
Sodium	6378 mg

* Percent Daily Values are based on a 2,000 calorie diet.

Chili I

Ingredients

- 1 tsp vegetable oil
- 2 boneless, skinless chicken breast halves
- 1 tsp vegetable oil
- 1 large onion, diced
- salt and freshly ground black pepper to taste
- 4 cloves garlic, chopped
- 1 tbsp ancho chile powder
- 1 tsp ground cumin
- 1 tsp all-purpose flour
- 1/2 tsp chipotle pepper powder
- 1/3 C. chopped fresh cilantro
- 1/4 tsp dried oregano
- 1 tsp fine cornmeal
- 2 C. chicken broth, divided
- 2 (15 oz.) cans white beans, drained
- 1 C. chicken broth
- 1/4 tsp white sugar, or to taste
- 1 pinch cayenne pepper, or to taste
- 1/3 C. chopped green onions
- 1/3 C. sour cream

Directions

- Sear your chicken in veggie oil (1 tsp) for 5 mins then lower the heat and turn over the chicken.

- Cook for 1 more min before placing a lid on the pot and cooking for 4 more mins.
- Ensure the chicken is fully done then cube the chicken after it has cooled off.
- Add in another tsp of oil to the pot and stir fry your onions for 7 mins then add some pepper and salt.
- Combine in the garlic and cook for 2 more mins.
- Now add: oregano, chili powder, chipotle powder, cumin, and flour.
- Cook for 3 mins then add the 1 C. of broth and scrape the browned bits in the bottom of the pan.
- Add the cornmeal and get it boiling.
- Once everything is boiling add the beans and another C. of broth.
- Lower the heat and gently cook the contents.
- Now add the chicken back in along with: cayenne, another C. of broth, sugar, salt, and black pepper.
- Heat everything up and then shut the heat.
- Let the content sit for about 2 mins.
- When serving, add a topping of cilantro, onions, and a dollop of sour cream.
- Enjoy.

Amount per serving (4 total)

Timing Information:

Preparation	20 m
Cooking	30 m
Total Time	50 m

Nutritional Information:

Calories	410 kcal
Fat	8.9 g
Carbohydrates	54.7g
Protein	29.1 g
Cholesterol	41 mg
Sodium	772 mg

* Percent Daily Values are based on a 2,000 calorie diet.

Restaurant Style Chicken II

Ingredients

- 2 large skinless, boneless chicken breast halves
- salt and black pepper to taste
- 8 asparagus spears, trimmed - divided
- 1/2 C. shredded mozzarella cheese, divided
- 1/4 C. Italian seasoned bread crumbs

Directions

- Coat a casserole dish with oil or nonstick spray and then set your oven to 375 degrees before doing anything else.
- With a mallet pound out your chicken breast on a working surface then top everything with pepper and salt.
- Put 4 pieces of asparagus in the middle of each, then a quarter of a C. of cheese.
- Shape the chicken into rolls then layer them in the casserole dish with the seam portion facing downwards.
- Top each one with 2 tbsps of bread crumbs.
- Cook everything in the oven for 30 mins.
- Enjoy.

Amount per serving (2 total)

Timing Information:

Preparation	20 m
Cooking	25 m
Total Time	45 m

Nutritional Information:

Calories	390 kcal
Fat	10.8 g
Carbohydrates	13.3g
Protein	57.4 g
Cholesterol	1147 mg
Sodium	581 mg

* Percent Daily Values are based on a 2,000 calorie diet.

Artisan Style Chicken with Artichokes

Ingredients

- 1 C. whole wheat or white flour
- 1/2 tsp salt
- 1/8 tsp white pepper, or to taste
- 1/8 tsp black pepper, or to taste
- 2 lbs chicken breast tenderloins or strips
- 2 tbsps canola oil
- 2 tbsps extra-virgin olive oil
- 2 C. chicken broth
- 2 tbsps fresh lemon juice
- 1 (12 oz.) jar quartered marinated artichoke hearts, with liquid
- 1/4 C. capers
- 2 tbsps butter
- 1/4 C. chopped flat-leaf parsley

Directions

- Get a bowl, mix: black pepper, flour, white pepper, and salt.
- Coat your chicken with the flour mix then fry them in olive and canola oil until fully done. Then place to the side.

- Now pour in lemon juice and broth then get it simmering and then add in the capers and artichokes.
- Get it simmering again.
- Continue to simmer with a low level of heat until half of the liquid has evaporated.
- Add the butter into the mix and let it melt before adding back in the chicken and simmering for 3 mins.
- Serve the chicken with some parsley and a liberal amount of sauce.
- Enjoy.

Amount per serving (6 total)

Timing Information:

Preparation	20 m
Cooking	20 m
Total Time	40 m

Nutritional Information:

Calories	408 kcal
Fat	18.6 g
Carbohydrates	22g
Protein	40.1 g
Cholesterol	98 mg
Sodium	719 mg

* Percent Daily Values are based on a 2,000 calorie diet.

Stuffed Chicken Breast IX

(Honey Mustard, Brown Mustard, and Ham)

Ingredients

- 4 skinless, boneless chicken breast halves
- 4 slices deli ham
- 3/4 C. shredded mozzarella cheese
- 3/4 C. honey
- 1/4 C. spicy brown mustard
- 1/4 C. yellow mustard

Directions

- Coat a casserole dish with nonstick spray and then set your oven to 375 degrees before doing anything else.
- With a mallet flatten your pieces of chicken then place a piece of ham and an equal amount of cheese on each.
- Now roll up the chicken and stake a toothpick through it.
- Layer the chicken pieces in the casserole dish.

- Get a bowl, combine: yellow mustard, honey, and brown mustard.
- Top the chicken with this mix and place a wrapping of foil around the dish as well.
- Cook everything in the oven for 45 mins.
- Enjoy.

Amount per serving (4 total)

Timing Information:

Preparation	15 m
Cooking	40 m
Total Time	55 m

Nutritional Information:

Calories	471 kcal
Fat	13 g
Carbohydrates	54.6g
Protein	36.6 g
Cholesterol	97 mg
Sodium	928 mg

* Percent Daily Values are based on a 2,000 calorie diet.

CHILI II

Ingredients

- 1/2 C. shredded Cheddar cheese
- 1/4 C. chopped green bell pepper
- 1/4 C. chopped red bell pepper
- 1/4 C. minced cilantro
- 1/4 C. diced tomatoes
- 1/2 tsp chili powder
- 1/2 tsp ground cumin
- 1/8 tsp salt
- 4 skinless, boneless chicken breast halves - flattened
- toothpicks

Directions

- Get a bowl, combine: salt, tomatoes, cumin, cheddar, chili powder, cilantro, red and green peppers.
- Dip your chicken breasts in the mix and then roll them up.
- Place a toothpick in each piece of chicken and put the rolls in the slow cooker.

- Add the rest of the mix to the slow cooker and then cook everything for 90 mins with high heat.
- Enjoy.

Amount per serving (4 total)

Timing Information:

Preparation	20 m
Cooking	3 h
Total Time	3 h 20 m

Nutritional Information:

Calories	199 kcal
Fat	8.3 g
Carbohydrates	2.1g
Protein	27.6 g
Cholesterol	79 mg
Sodium	259 mg

* Percent Daily Values are based on a 2,000 calorie diet.

Goat Cheese and Balsamic Chicken Breast

Ingredients

- 1 tsp olive oil
- 1 shallot, finely diced
- 1 C. balsamic vinegar
- 2 skinless, boneless chicken breast halves
- 2 oz. goat cheese, divided

Directions

- Set your oven to 350 degrees before doing anything else.
- Stir fry your shallots in olive oil for 7 mins then add in the balsamic and cook for 12 mins while stirring with a low heat and a gentle boil.
- With a mallet flatten your chicken pieces then add: half of the cheese, and 1/3 of the balsamic mix.
- Roll up the chicken pieces around the mix and then stake a toothpick through each before layering them all in a casserole dish.
- Pour the rest of the balsamic over the chicken in the dish and then cook everything in the oven for 40 mins. Enjoy.

Amount per serving (2 total)

Timing Information:

Preparation	15 m
Cooking	30 m
Total Time	45 m

Nutritional Information:

Calories	340 kcal
Fat	13.5 g
Carbohydrates	23.5g
Protein	30.1 g
Cholesterol	83 mg
Sodium	230 mg

* Percent Daily Values are based on a 2,000 calorie diet.

THANKS FOR READING! JOIN THE CLUB AND KEEP ON COOKING WITH 6 MORE COOKBOOKS....

http://bit.ly/1TdrStv

 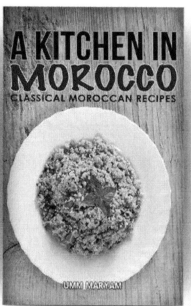 

To grab the box sets simply follow the link mentioned above, or tap one of book covers.

This will take you to a page where you can simply enter your email address and a PDF version of the box sets will be emailed to you.

Hope you are ready for some serious cooking!

http://bit.ly/1TdrStv

Come On...
Let's Be Friends :)

We adore our readers and love connecting with them socially.

Like BookSumo on Facebook and let's get social!

Facebook

And also check out the BookSumo Cooking Blog.

Food Lover Blog

Printed in Great Britain
by Amazon